S0-BSZ-455

CHOPPERS

MotoR Mania

by Matt Doeden

Joe Leonard, consultant

Lerner Publications Company • Minneapolis

Cover Photo: This is a 1997 Harley-Davidson Fat Boy chopper called Twisted Reality.

Copyright © 2008 by Lerner Publishing Group, Inc.

Lerner Publications Company
A division of Lerner Publishing Group, Inc.
241 First Avenue North
Minneapolis, MN 55401 U.S.A.

Website address: www.lernerbooks.com

Library of Congress Cataloging-in-Publication Data

Doeden, Matt.
    Choppers / by Matt Doeden.
        p.   cm. — (Motor mania)
    Includes bibliographical references and index.
    ISBN 978–0–8225–7288–6 (lib. bdg. : alk. paper)
    1. Choppers (Motorcycles)—Juvenile literature. 2. Motorcycles—Customizing—Juvenile literature.
    I. Title.
    TL440.15.D635 2008
    629.227'5—dc22   2007026099

Manufactured in the United States of America
1 2 3 4 5 6 – DP – 13 12 11 10 09 08

Contents

WHAT IS A CHOPPER?

A chopper is much more than just a motorcycle. It is a work of art and a way to say something about yourself. To many, the chopper stands for freedom and a sense of adventure. Chopper owners don't just want any factory-made motorcycle. They want a machine that will show off who they are.

It's difficult to say exactly what makes a chopper. All choppers are motorcycles that have been changed from the factory setup. A chopper usually has a long front fork, which holds the front wheel. The long fork gives the motorcycle a tough look. A fat rear tire adds to this look. Many owners take off unnecessary parts to make the bikes as light as possible. Finally, no chopper is complete without a custom paint job.

Any kind of motorcycle can be made into a chopper. Harley-Davidson motorcycles, though, are the huge favorites among chopper owners. Other kinds of choppers are based on everything from American-made Indian motorcycles to new European and Japanese bikes. The biggest key is that every chopper is a rare, one-of-a-kind machine.

This chopper was on display at a bike rally in 2006.

Chapter One

CHOPPER HISTORY

Motorcycles have been a popular way to get around for more than 100 years. In the late 1860s, trains and ships offered travel to large groups of people.

The first powered two-wheeled vehicle ran on steam. This machine could reach speeds of 10 miles (16 kilometers) per hour, but it had no brakes.

But for those who wished to go where they pleased, when they pleased, the horse was the only option. In 1868 Sylvester H. Roper of Massachusetts set out to change that. He built a two-wheeled vehicle that looked a little like a bicycle. The machine ran on the power of a small steam engine. Roper's creation was one of the inventions that led to the modern motorcycle.

The idea of a powered two-wheel vehicle didn't take off at first. But Roper and other inventors continued to improve on the design.

Gasoline-powered engines soon replaced steam power. In the mid-1880s, Gottlieb Daimler attached an internal combustion (gasoline) engine to a wood-framed machine. The machine had two main wheels. There were also two smaller wheels that helped with balance. Most agree that Daimler's invention was the first true motorcycle.

German engineer Gottlieb Daimler *(left)* invented the first modern gasoline-powered motorcycle *(above).*

The 1901 Werner

Built by brothers Michel and Eugene Werner, the 1901 Werner helped make motorcycles popular. The model was strong and steady. It helped people see the motorcycle as a reliable form of transportation.

Despite its good reputation, the 1901 Werner had plenty of problems. The engine would only run when the motorcycle was in motion. The brakes worked poorly. Worst of all, the engine didn't have enough power to go up most hills. The motorcycle included pedals for the rider to use to help in the climb.

William S. Harley and brothers Arthur and Walter Davidson built their first motorcycle in 1903. Their company, Harley–Davidson, would go on to become a giant in the industry and a huge part of chopper culture.

Over the next few decades, motorcycles became more popular. Along with automobiles, motorcycles replaced horses as a way for people to get around. Something about the freedom of riding on two wheels appealed to people. Automobiles of the time were big and clunky. To many people, motorcycles seemed easier and more fun to drive. Soon, motorcycles were all over. They could be found on the road, speeding around racetracks, or jumping off tall ramps. They were even used in the military.

Meanwhile, the American motorcycle maker Harley-Davidson was becoming one of the leaders in the industry. The company began making motorcycles in Milwaukee, Wisconsin, in 1903. In its first year, Harley-Davidson built just 50 bikes. Within three years, that number had jumped to 1,100. By 1919 the company

The Harley-Davidson company popularized the V-twin engine *(above)*, which is still a part of Harley motorcycles. Below: Walter Davidson, the first president of Harley-Davidson Motor Company, stands with one of the first motorcycles built by the company.

was building more than 23,000 bikes a year. In the United States, only the Indian Motorcycle Company was making more motorcycles at the time.

Harley-Davidsons were popular because they were fast, tough, and not too expensive. The motorcycle's most identifying feature soon became the V-twin engine, which appeared on Harley bikes in 1909. This is a type of engine in which two cylinders are placed in the shape of a V. The engine was smooth and powerful and remains a part of Harley designs.

Internal Combustion Engines

Like most cars, motorcycles have internal combustion engines. Internal combustion engines run on gasoline. Most motorcycles have a four-stroke cycle that burns a mixture of air and gas to power the machine *(right)*. Internal combustion engines provide a lot of power to a vehicle. They were a big improvement over the first powered two-wheel vehicles that used steam engines.

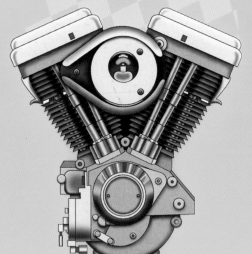

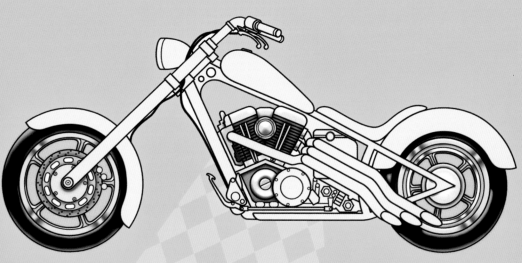

1. INTAKE STROKE
The piston moves down the cylinder and draws the fuel-air mixture into the cylinder through the intake valve.

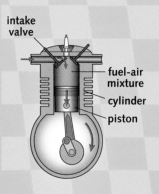

intake valve

fuel-air mixture

cylinder

piston

2. COMPRESSION STROKE
The piston moves up and compresses the fuel-air mixture. The spark plug ignites the mixture, creating combustion (burning).

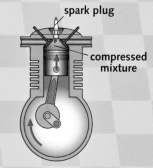

spark plug

compressed mixture

3. POWER STROKE
The burning gases created by combustion push the piston downward. This gives the engine its power.

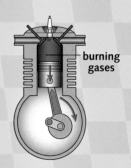

burning gases

4. EXHAUST STROKE
The piston moves up again and pushes out the burned-out exhaust gases through the exhaust valve.

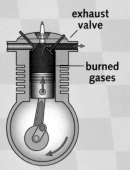

exhaust valve

burned gases

The Bobber

By the 1940s, motorcycles were common in the United States. Following the lead of automobile fans, many bikers had begun to customize their rides to suit their needs. Some of these changes were just for looks. Other changes improved the bikes' performance (a vehicle's speed and handling).

After World War II (1939–1945), many U.S. soldiers returned to the United States. Some of them had ridden military motorcycles in Europe and wanted

A U.S. Army Harley–Davidson motorcycle used in the early 1940s

one of their own back home. But the U.S.-built motorcycles of the time were much different from the easy-to-ride bikes they'd had in Europe. The most popular brands in the United States were big, bulky Indians and Harley-Davidsons. These bikes seemed clumsy and awkward to the soldiers. Because of this, many returning soldiers bought extra military motorcycles left over after the war.

Soon many of these riders were customizing their motorcycles. They worked on Harleys, Indians, and military bikes alike. They changed the motorcycles to make them lighter and easier to handle. One of the major changes many owners made was to "bob" (cut down) the bike's big fenders. This gave the motorcycle a smaller, sleeker look and a smoother ride. Some owners simply took off the rear fender. They replaced it with the motorcycle's smaller front fender. They also removed any parts that seemed too big or unnecessary.

This Triumph motorcycle was customized in the 1970s.

The Honda CB750, built in Japan, was one of the fastest bikes of the 1960s.

Meanwhile, they replaced other parts such as gas tanks with smaller versions. They called the bikes bobbers. These sleek, customized machines would later lead to the first choppers.

The bobber remained popular throughout the 1950s and into the early 1960s. The most popular motorcycle to turn into a bobber was a Harley-Davidson. A typical bobber included small footpegs and no turn signals. A small front tire and a fat rear tire were also important. Chrome-plated parts became popular, giving the motorcycles a shiny appearance. A low seat and high handlebars completed the bobber look.

The Modern Chopper Emerges

By the 1960s, American bikers had discovered that their bobbers weren't the fastest motorcycles around anymore. The Japanese-built Honda CB750 was blowing the U.S.-made custom bikes out of the water. Several British bikes also had more speed.

A few changes would allow bobbers to be driven at higher speeds while still keeping them safe. American riders lengthened the front ends of their motorcycles. Many customizers began adding long forks to push the front wheel farther and farther forward. As the forks grew longer, the rake of the bikes increased. A motorcycle's rake is the degree of the angle of its fork. For example, if the angle between the fork and a straight line extending up was 40 degrees, the bike was said to have a 40-degree rake. Long forks also made a longer wheelbase. The wheelbase is the distance between the front and rear wheels. Increasing a motorcycle's wheelbase was called stretching. This provided a smoother, safer ride at high speeds.

Customizers started adding longer and longer forks to motorcycles in the 1960s. Long forks, like this one, became one of the identifying features of a chopper.

There are long forks, and then there are *long* forks. The fork of this Japanese chopper is a jaw-dropping 12.5 feet (3.8 meters)!

The downside to a stretched motorcycle was that the bikes were harder to control at slow speeds. But owners liked the look of the long fork. They loved zooming down the highway on their long, stretched-out motorcycles. These bikes became known as choppers because of the way that owners stripped, or chopped, all the unnecessary parts. Any motorcycle could be turned into a chopper. But Harley-Davidsons were still the favorite choice. Bikers loved the Harley's strong look and tough construction.

By this time, the chopper had become a statement of personal style. Chopper owners took pride in their stretched-out, stripped-down machines. The design of the chopper was intimidating to many. It became a symbol of rebellion. Basic factory-built bikes weren't good enough for chopper owners. They

Ape Hangers

Some people call the chopper's usual high handlebars "ape hangers" *(left)*. A rider holding the handlebars reaches so high up that he resembles an ape holding onto a tree branch.

wanted something that stood out as unique and maybe even a little bit dangerous.

For decades, bobber and chopper culture had been mainly an underground hobby. It was not widely popular or even understood by most people. Many didn't even really know what a chopper was. But in 1969, the movie *Easy Rider* changed all that.

Easy Rider told the story of two friends riding their motorcycles from Los Angeles, California, to New Orleans, Louisiana. The film's star, Peter Fonda, rode a Harley-Davidson chopper called *Captain America*. The motorcycle had the usual long fork. It also had a tall sissy bar that rose high above the rider's shoulders. The sissy

bar helped the rider to comfortably lean back in the seat. *Captain America*'s most famous feature, however, was its custom stars-and-stripes paint job.

Fonda's machine stole the show. Suddenly, the demand for choppers soared. Almost overnight, the culture of the chopper had changed forever.

Together, Peter Fonda and his chopper, *Captain America*, helped bring the chopper culture into the mainstream.

The Evolving Chopper

As the demand for choppers rose, the business of customized motorcycles also grew. New magazines such as *Street Chopper*, *Hot Bike*, and *Chopper Magazine* turned up on newsstands. They included articles about and photos of customized bikes. They also had tips on how to make your own chopper. Meanwhile, shops that helped people customize motorcycles began to spring up all over the United States. Those who wanted to build their own choppers no longer had to start from scratch. Custom parts could be ordered from around the country.

Ordering parts through the mail made customizing much easier.

The style of chopper popular in the late 1960s and 1970s is often called the early, or traditional, chopper. Most were based on Harley-Davidsons or Honda 750 Fours. A key feature of these bikes is that they were set up without any springs, or shock absorbers, in the rear suspension

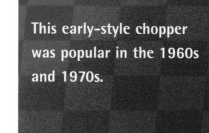

This early-style chopper was popular in the 1960s and 1970s.

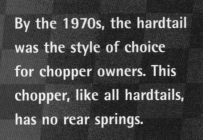

By the 1970s, the hardtail was the style of choice for chopper owners. This chopper, like all hardtails, has no rear springs.

system. The rear suspension system is the set of parts that connect the back wheel to the main part of a motorcycle. This style had been around for decades. But in the late 1960s and 1970s, more and more choppers adopted the look. Bikes with this customization were called hardtails. The rigid look of the hardtail became very popular. Soon it

was difficult to find a chopper that included rear springs. Even the choppers that weren't hardtails were set up to look as if they were.

Fuel prices rose during the 1970s. As a result, motorcycling grew even more popular. Motorcycles didn't use as much gas as the big, fuel-hogging cars that were common at the time. Many people who turned to motorcycles to save money would discover the joys of customized bikes.

The Harley-Davidson company struggled in the late 1970s and early 1980s. Motorcycles were still very popular. But Harley's bikes could not compete with

the cheaper motorcycles that Japanese companies were building. For a while, the legendary bike maker was in danger of shutting down its factory forever. But in 1983, the U.S. government placed an increased tax on foreign-built motorcycles. The price of these bikes rose in the United States. The tax gave Harley-Davidson a chance to compete. The law was passed mainly as a way to save Harley-Davidson. It was the only motorcycle maker in the United States at the time. The tax, along with better ways of making motorcycles, put Harley-Davidson back on top.

Meanwhile, motorcycle styles were changing. For example, big rear tires had always been common on classic choppers. But during the 1980s, this style became even more extreme.

Japanese-made motorcycles, like this Kawasaki Z900, dominated the market in the late 1970s and early 1980s.

This Harley-Davidson chopper displays many common chopper features. Note the ultrawide rear tire.

The bikes looked great with the ultra-wide rear tires. They also helped riders control the bikes at high speeds. But the fat tires also made the choppers hard to control at slow speeds and in tight spaces. Still, many bikers were happy with the look. Choppers had become more about style than speed and handling. Superbikes were for those who wanted the fastest motorcycles. Superbikes are compact motorcycles built mainly for speed. More than ever, choppers were about looks and attitude.

In recent years, the old bobber-style has made a comeback. These old-school bikes share much in common with modern choppers. But they don't have the long forks and stretched-out look that have come to define the classic chopper.

A Renewed Interest

In the late 1990s and early 2000s, many people became interested in car customizing. Television programs such as *Monster Garage* showed people building strange and beautiful custom cars. But while custom car shows were popular, none were as popular as *American Chopper*, which first appeared on Discovery Channel in 2003.

As *American Chopper* soared in popularity, so too did the status of choppers. Suddenly, it seemed everyone wanted a customized motorcycle. For decades, chopper owners were seen as rebels. Almost overnight, though, it seemed that people from all walks of life became interested in choppers. Customizing shops such as Orange County Choppers and West Coast Choppers were flooded with orders. Stunning new designs were turning up all over. Choppers were bigger than ever.

Paul Teutul Sr. is a star of *American Chopper* and the owner of Orange County Choppers.

Chapter Two

CHOPPER CULTURE

Scott Ellis shows off his customized chopper at the Americade motorcycle rally in Lake George, New York, in June 2006.

The culture of choppers is similar to that of custom car lovers. Both chopper owners and custom car builders see their vehicles as more than just ways to get around. Each one is a work of art and a source of pride for its maker. Choppers no longer stand for the same sense of rebellion that they did in the past. But to many, they're still a great way to express the personality of the builder.

Yet for true chopper fans, there's more to it than that. Choppers aren't just works of art to be driven to shows and parades. They're symbols of freedom. Chopper owners love nothing

better than hitting the open road on a beautiful bike that they helped create.

Types of Custom Bikes

Chopper owners tend to like a special style of bike. Some prefer the classic look of the 1950s bobbers. Custom bikes made in this mold are called old school. Owners trim down the fenders and remove all the parts that they can. They enjoy the light, stripped-down feel of the motorcycle.

Others prefer the form of the classic chopper. These early bikes have the look that was popular in the 1960s. They include long forks, a stretched

Almost every part of this radical chopper has been customized.

wheelbase, and additions such as sissy bars. Radical choppers, meanwhile, often have wild paint jobs and expensive premade parts. Radicals are often more for show than for riding. But their owners still prize long forks and extreme rake angles.

In recent years, other classes of customized motorcycles have grown in popularity. Compact streetfighter bikes focus on pure speed. Smooth handling and control make pro street bikes popular. For motorcycle fans, there's a wide range of models from which to choose. Choppers became popular in part because of their owners' desires to have the meanest, fastest bikes on the planet. But recent choppers can't compete with some of the newer models in speed and handling.

Building a Chopper

There is no clear definition of exactly what a chopper is. But a set of common features does seem to define the usual chopper. It has a long fork and a low seat. The frame has a rigid look. Most choppers are hardtails. Most also have a V-twin engine. From there, the bikes vary widely. Some owners add every detail and feature they can. These might include custom paint jobs or chrome-plated parts. Others prefer the simpler, stripped-down look of the first bobbers and choppers.

V-Twin Engine

In 1994 Harley-Davidson tried to file a trademark (exclusive rights to a symbol) for the famous deep rumble of its V-twin engine *(right)*. But other motorcycle manufacturers fought the trademark, and Harley-Davidson eventually withdrew the application.

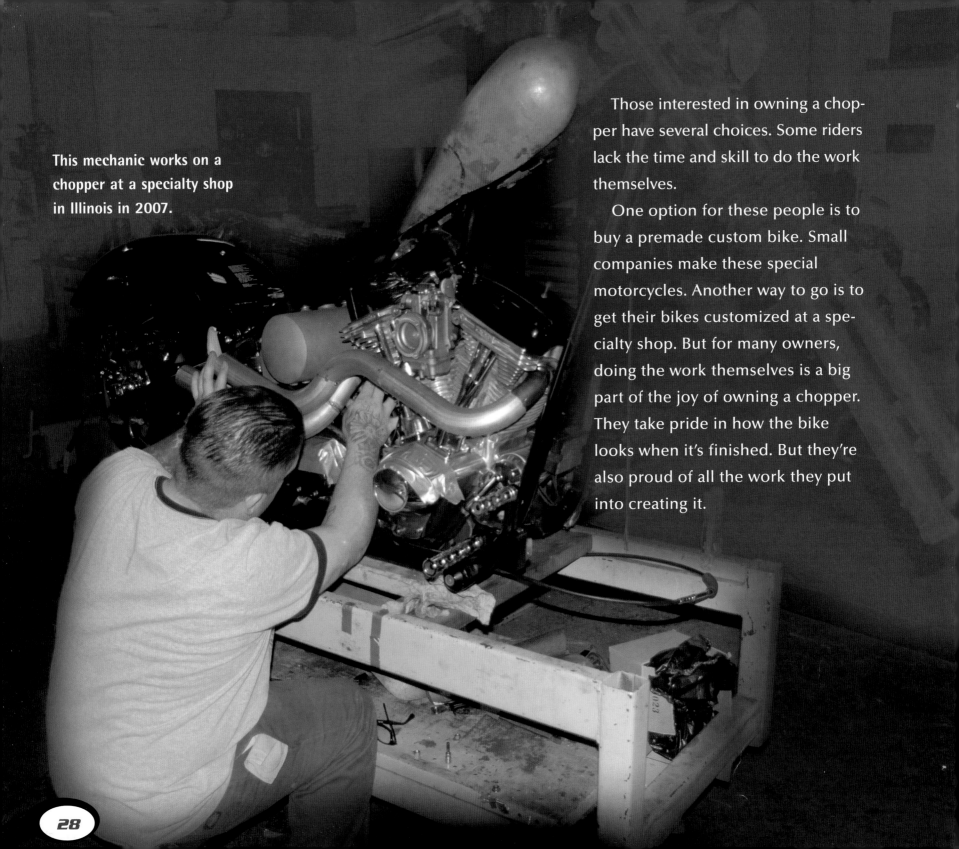

This mechanic works on a chopper at a specialty shop in Illinois in 2007.

Those interested in owning a chopper have several choices. Some riders lack the time and skill to do the work themselves.

One option for these people is to buy a premade custom bike. Small companies make these special motorcycles. Another way to go is to get their bikes customized at a specialty shop. But for many owners, doing the work themselves is a big part of the joy of owning a chopper. They take pride in how the bike looks when it's finished. But they're also proud of all the work they put into creating it.

DID YOU KNOW?

For decades Harley-Davidson was the only major motorcycle manufacturer in the United States. But in 1998, the Minnesota-based Victory Motorcycles began production. Victory was started by the company that makes Polaris snowmobiles. One of Victory's motorcycles is shown at left.

Since the chopper craze of the late 1990s and early 2000s, it's easier than ever to build a custom motorcycle. Dozens of books and magazines guide new owners through the process. Catalogs and websites sell thousands of different parts and accessories. Websites also offer all kinds of help. Step-by-step instructions and communities where people share advice can both be found on the Internet.

The first step in building a chopper is to choose the perfect type of motorcycle. For decades Harley-Davidsons have been the choice of most builders. Other brands, though, have grown in popularity. For example, some of the most exciting new choppers are built around less-expensive Honda or Kawasaki frames. It's all a matter of personal taste and budget. The classic Harley-Davidson chopper will always be a favorite. But some people prefer to go their own way. After all, personal style is part of the fun of owning a chopper.

Taking the bike out on the open road is a must for most chopper enthusiasts.

The next task is to plan the customization. Many builders spend hours looking at finished choppers in magazines and in person. They find the features they like and map out a plan for a safe but striking machine. Builders can find parts at specialty shops. Parts are also available through catalogs or on the Internet.

Some people like to customize their bikes from scratch. They buy each part separately. Others buy special kits that include everything a builder would need. These kits don't offer many options. But they can be of great help to first-time builders.

With a plan in place, it's time to begin the work. Builders may replace the bike's fork and add a fat rear tire. They may give the bike a unique paint job with a candy (shiny) finish. Footpegs and sissy bars are common additions. Some even add ape-hanger handlebars and high-rising king-and-queen seats.

When a chopper is finished, it's time to hit the road. The joy of building a custom motorcycle is a big part of the fun. But while some builders make choppers just for show, most agree that the bikes are made to be ridden. Some ride alone, while others go with a group of friends. Either way, taking it onto the road is what the chopper lifestyle is all about.

Showing Off

For many, just riding a chopper on the open road is enough. The image of Peter Fonda on *Captain America* brings to mind the sense of freedom many owners feel. But for some, riding isn't the best part of owning a chopper. For them, a big part of the joy is getting together with other bikers and showing off their creations. Some do this at car and motorcycle shows. Others prefer large gatherings called rallies.

A replica of the Harley-Davidson chopper Peter Fonda rode in *Easy Rider*.

Custom car shows have been around for more than half a century. In the 1960s, these events began springing up all over the United States. Owners displayed hot rods, street rods, and other types of custom cars. Before long, chopper builders were joining the shows. But motorcycle people are an independent breed. Soon they were having shows of their own.

Choppers are displayed at this motorcycle show in 2005.

Shows are great places for motorcycle fans to gather. The events usually include booths and displays that show the latest in chopper technology. There may be guest speakers and demonstrations. But the stars of the shows are the custom motorcycles themselves. Individuals and customizing shops display their bikes. They show everything from old-school models to crazy new radicals. It's a great place for bikers to see what others are doing. Best of all, it gives fans a chance to get together and talk about choppers.

Some bikers prefer to gather in more relaxed settings. Motorcycle rallies are less formal than shows. They're a great way for bikers to gather and just hang out with their bikes. Some rallies include just a dozen friends and their choppers. Others attract tens of thousands of strangers. Either way, it's a great place to show off a bike and soak in the motorcycle culture.

This street in a Florida town is lined with motorcycles during a rally in 2003.

WELCOME RIDERS!

The Sturgis Motorcycle Rally in South Dakota is the king of all motorcycle rallies. In 2006 about 450,000 people flocked to Sturgis to enjoy the festivities.

Sturgis

In the late 1930s, South Dakota's Clarence "Pappy" Hoel started the Jackpine Gypsies Motorcycle Club. Hoel, who rode an Indian motorcycle, wanted to hold a race in Sturgis. That first year, just nine riders participated in Hoel's race.

Over the decades, word spread about the yearly event in Sturgis. As the chopper culture boomed in the 1970s, so too did the popularity of Sturgis. Soon, for one week each summer, the small town was overwhelmed by motorcyclists. By the 2000s, the rally had grown into an enormous event, attracting bikers from around the world. Although Sturgis has gained a reputation as having a wild, partying atmosphere, for most people the rally is all about the motorcycles. It's a great place to see a huge variety of choppers.

The world's most famous motorcycle rally is held each year in Sturgis, South Dakota. The Sturgis Motorcycle Rally was first held in the late 1930s. It has since grown into the biggest motorcycle event in the world. In the 2000s, it's not unusual to have almost half a million people attend the event. Many of them arrive on their bikes. Sturgis is open to both factory-built and custom motorcycles. But choppers and other customized bikes are always some of the most popular attractions.

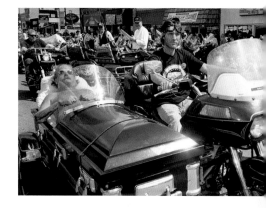

Motorcycles of all shapes and sizes can be seen at Sturgis. The motorcycle above has a sidecar that looks like a coffin, while the choppers below get plenty of attention.

Jesse James holds his book, *I am Jesse James*, at a book signing at his West Coast Choppers showroom in 2004. He is also the star of the popular television show *Monster Garage*.

A New Culture

Chopper culture went through a huge change in the early 2000s. This was due to the success of a few car and motorcycle customizing TV shows. This new kind of reality show was made popular by Discovery Channel's *Monster Garage*. The show first aired in 2002. It gave viewers a behind-the-scenes look at customization.

Monster Garage focused on cars. But the show did touch on other vehicles, including boats and motorcycles. In fact, the show's star, Jesse James, is a famous motorcycle builder. He is the owner of the famous shop West Coast Choppers.

American Chopper took things a step further in 2003. The show was based on events that took place in the Orange County Choppers motorcycle shop. It was an instant hit. Shop owner Paul Teutul Sr. was known for his screaming, practical jokes, and wild behavior. He became the star of the show. American Chopper focused on Teutul and his employees almost as much as it did on the stunning machines they were creating. The mix appealed to viewers, and the show enjoyed much success.

Hit shows like American Chopper created a wave of interest in customized motorcycles. Demand for the machines soared. Some chopper

Left to right: Paul Teutul Sr. and his sons, Paul Teutul Jr. and Mikey Teutul, are all stars of the successful TV show *American Chopper.*

Radicals

As custom bikes have grown wilder and more expensive, new kinds of choppers have emerged. For example, many radicals are so expensive to build that owners rarely take them on the road. Many of these bikes are built just for show.

fans were thrilled with all the attention. Others were not. The spirit of freedom that had long been associated with choppers was slowly disappearing. Trends were changing. The kinds of people who owned the machines began to shift. Many of these new bikers had spent tens of thousands of dollars on their customized choppers. They didn't want to ride their bikes and risk damaging the chrome finishes and expensive paint jobs. Clearly, the culture had come a long way from the days when choppers were all about riding on the open road.

At Sturgis in the early 2000s, many longtime bikers really noticed the change. Suddenly, lots of small trailers appeared at the rally. People were loading their motorcycles onto the trailers and hauling them out to

A man dusts off his motorcycle after the trip from Texas to South Dakota for the 2006 Sturgis Motorcycle Rally. More people are transporting their motorcycles to events on trailers, rather than riding them.

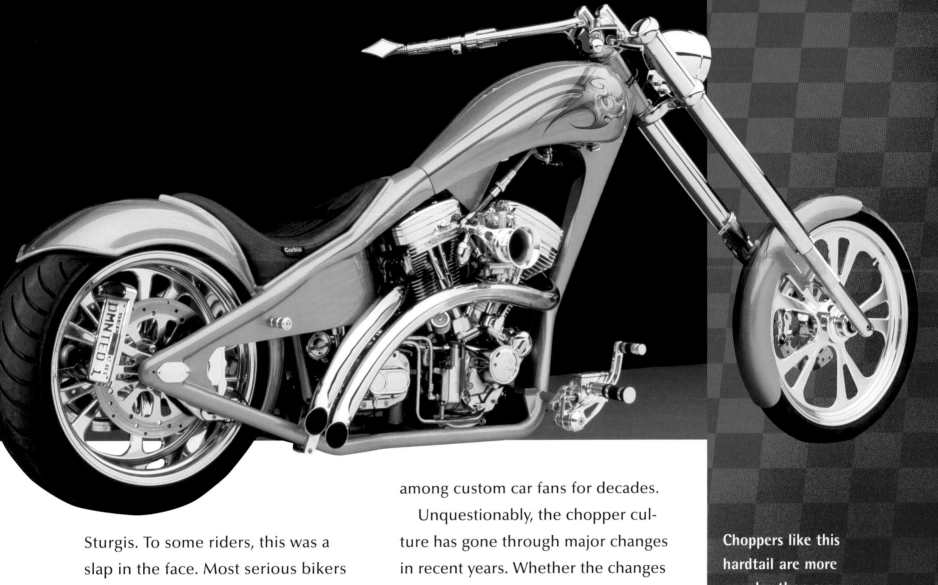

Sturgis. To some riders, this was a slap in the face. Most serious bikers agree that owning a motorcycle is about the journey, not the destination. The new class of bikers, they said, didn't understand that. For the first time, the motorcycle culture was going through the show-versus-go debate. This argument had raged among custom car fans for decades.

Unquestionably, the chopper culture has gone through major changes in recent years. Whether the changes are good or bad is debatable. But a couple of things are certain. The interest in choppers and other customized motorcycles has never been higher. And for many, the chopper remains a rare symbol of freedom and personal style.

Choppers like this hardtail are more popular than ever.

Captain America

One of two motorcycles originally built for *Easy Rider*, *Captain America* is easily the most famous chopper in history. Although *Captain America* was wrecked during filming, it was carefully rebuilt and is on display at the National Motorcycle Museum in Anamosa, Iowa.

El Balla

El Balla, which translates to "the Whale," is an example of how different a radical can be. Taking a page out of the culture of lowrider cars, this ride has an adjustable suspension. The rider can raise the bike while on the road and lower it for an extra mean look at shows.

Tramp

If you're looking for an extralong fork and an extreme rake, *Tramp* is the kind of bike for you. This radical old-school chopper boasts a 32-inch telescopic fork. The classic look is highlighted by its flat black paint and liberal use of chrome throughout.

El

El combines the old-fashioned line of a bobber with some of the souped-up features of an early chopper. The gentle 34-degree rake and generally stripped-down look bring to mind a 1950s bobber, but the lacquered paint job and ape-hanger handlebars, among other features, come straight out of the chopper culture.

Retro Chopper

As the popularity of choppers has soared, a class of factory pre-built bikes has boomed. These bikes have the unique features of a customized chopper but come straight from the factory. *Retro Chopper* is a great example. Its sleek lines and curves leave no doubt that its as modern as choppers come.

Purple Haze

This chopper, built around a 1955 Harley, is a lean and mean bike. Owner Michael Bailey first bought the bike in 1974, but it wasn't until the 1990s that he customized it. The job took him two years, but *Purple Haze*'s slick, one-of-a-kind look was well worth the effort.

Outlaw

Not all early choppers were built around Harley-Davidsons—and *Outlaw* makes the case. The bike, built from a Triumph Bonneville in the 1970s, had fallen into disrepair. But once restored, complete with its purple and yellow paint job and a shortened chrome rear fender, *Outlaw* has a look all its own.

Hundred Grand

Radicals are unlike any other type of motorcycle. *Hundred Grand* is a great example of how different—and how expensive—a radical can be. Its ultralow seat, curved lines, and extreme rake are just the beginning. Closer inspection reveals that the rearview mirrors have been replaced by a camera and video screen. This is one high-tech chopper!

Rigid

Rigid, named for its hardtail setup, is a throwback custom motorcycle. With the simplicity of an old-fashioned bobber, *Rigid* lacks the lacquered paint job and heavy chrome of many modern choppers.

Shady Lady

Shady Lady is proof that choppers aren't just for men. With its gentle 38-degree rake, pink flames, and small frame, this factory chopper is built for a woman. Even though this bike may look tame compared to other choppers, its big S&S engine provides plenty of punch.

Glossary

bobber: a style of motorcycle customization that involves cutting back the fenders and stripping unnecessary parts and sheet metal

chrome: a coating of a metallic substance called chromium that gives metal objects a shiny, new look

customize: to change a vehicle's appearance

early chopper: a motorcycle customized in the style of the first choppers

fork: the part of a motorcycle that holds the front tire

hardtail: a motorcycle that lacks a rear suspension system. Hardtail motorcycles are often referred to as rigid.

king and queen seat: a type of motorcycle seat that allows two people to ride on the same bike

old school: a motorcycle customized in the style of the classic bobber

radical: a motorcycle customized with expensive prefabricated parts, fancy custom paint jobs, and more

rake: the angle of a motorcycle's fork

softtail: a motorcycle that includes a rear suspension system

streetfighter: a type of superbike customized for maximum speed and performance

suspension system: a vehicle's system of springs and shock absorbers

tariff: a tax imposed on imported goods

V-twin: a type of motorcycle engine that includes two cylinders arranged in the shape of a V

Selected Bibliography

Dregni, Michael. *The Spirit of the Motorcycle*. Stillwater, MN: Voyageur Press, 2000.

Mitchel, Doug. *Choppers and Custom Motorcycles*. Lincolnwood, IL: Publications International, 2005.

Rafferty, Tod. *Harley-Davidson 100 Years: Celebration of a Legend*. Saint Paul: MBI Publishing, 2002.

Remus, Timothy. *How to Build a Cheap Chopper*. Stillwater, MN: Wolfgang Publications, 2004.

Further Reading

Girdler, Allan. *Harley-Davidson*. Saint Paul: MBI Publishing, 2006.

Goodman, Susan E., and Michael J. Doolittle. *Choppers*. New York: Random House, 2004.

Smedman, Lisa. *From Boneshakers to Choppers: The Rip-Roaring History of Motorcycles*. Toronto: Annick Press, 2007.

Websites

Choppers and Custom Cycles
http://www.choppers.com
Choppers.com is a website devoted to choppers. It includes photos, chopper news, show dates, links to dealers, and much more.

Harley-Davidson.com
http://www.harley-davidson.com
The home page of Harley-Davidson includes information about all of its factory-made motorcycles, with photos, specifications, and other information.

How Stuff Works—Motorcycles
http://auto.howstuffworks.com/motorcycle.htm
Howstuffworks.com's page on motorcycles gives the basics on how motorcycles are built and ridden.

Orange County Choppers
http://www.orangecountychoppers.com
This commercial site for the famous customizing shop includes news about Orange County Choppers and the *American Chopper* TV show.

Index

About the Author

Matt Doeden is a freelance author and editor living in Minnesota. He's written more than 50 children's books, including dozens on cars, motorcycles, and drivers.

About the Consultant

Joe Leonard is sales manager at Fury Motorcycles in South Saint Paul, Minnesota, a Big Dog Motorcycles dealership.

Photo Acknowledgments

The images in this book are used with permission of: © Piotr & Irena Kolasa/Alamy, pp. 4–5; © Mirrorpix/Courtesy Everett Collection, p. 6 (background); © SSPL/The Image Works, pp. 6 (bottom), 8; © Jacques Boyer/Roger-Viollet/The Image Works, p. 7 (top); © POPPERFOTO/ Alamy, p. 7 (bottom); © martin norris/Alamy, p. 9; © Lourens Smak/Alamy, p. 10 (top); © Bettmann/CORBIS, p. 10 (bottom); © Laura Westlund/Independent Picture Service, p. 11 (all); © wyrdlight/Alamy, p. 12; © Doug Mitchel, pp. 13, 19, 28, 41 (bottom), 42 (both), 43 (bottom), 44 (top), 45 (top); © Bernie Epstein/Alamy, p. 14; © Andre Jenny/Alamy, p. 15; © geldi/Alamy, p. 16; © Bert de Ruiter/Alamy, p. 17; "Easy Rider", © 1969, renewed 1997 Columbia Pictures Industries, Inc. All Rights Reserved. Courtesy of Columbia Pictures. Image courtesy of The Everett collection, p. 18; © Russ Austin/Precious Metal Customs, pp. 20, 25, 44 (bottom); © Motoring Picture Library/Alamy, p. 21; © Alan Stone/Alamy, p. 22; © Discovery Channel/Courtesy: Everett Collection, p. 23; © Alvaro Isidoro/Photonews/Camera Press/Retna Ltd., pp. 24 (background), 32; © Michael Doolittle/Alamy, pp. 24 (bottom), 29; © Chris Laurens/ Alamy, p. 26; © Martin Karius/Alamy, p. 27; © John Kelly/Iconica/Getty Images, p. 30; © HENNY RAY ABRAMS/AFP/Getty Images, p. 31; © PhotoStockFile/Alamy, p. 33; AP Photo/Morry Gash, p. 34; © FRANCIS TEMMAN/AFP/Getty Images, p. 35 (top); © Peter Turnley/CORBIS, p. 35 (bottom); AP Photo/Tammie Arroyo, p. 36; AP Photo/Rob Griffith, p. 37; AP Photo/Joe Kafka, p. 38; © Ron Kimball/Ron Kimball Stock, p. 39; © simon clay/Alamy, p. 41 (top); © 2007 Bourget's Bike Works, Inc., p. 43 (top); © Wicked Women Choppers, LLC. and John Mann, Chrome Pony, p. 45 (bottom).

Front cover: © Ron Kimball/Ron Kimball Stock